Soul Searching

Ambrosia Rainer

BookLeaf Publishing

Presentation by *BookLeaf Publishing*

Web: www.bookleafpub.com

E-mail: info@bookleafpub.com

ISBN: 9789357619721

First edition 2023

DEDICATION

I dedicate this book to everyone that is struggling to find themselves. If you've gotten lost along the way, if you are trying to make amends, if you are learning how to embrace yourself... this book is for you.

Never give up on yourself. Never settle if you know deep down, you can do better.

This book is dedicated to those of us that are trying to find our peace in a world full of hate.

Each day can be another step closer to living your dream. Just keep going and never stop dreaming.

Reality Check

Another year has came
and went
When you look back…
Can you say there was value
in the time you spent?
Where are you now?
Is it how you hoped?
or
Are you still putting on a smile,
doing it for show?
Did your dreams come true?
Are they a work in progress?
or
Have they been forgotten?
Buried deep within…
Can you say you're happy?
Are you satisfied?
Are you grateful for your life?
If it were all to end…
Would you have wanted more?
Was your heart content?
Would you Rest In Peace?
Is your soul at ease?
Have your demons been released?
Are you still holding on to things?

Hoping for a change
but never doing what it takes
to actually make a change?
What day is it?
Not of the week.
What day are you on
in your journey?
Are you exceeding expectations?
Doing what you said you was gonna do
without hesitation?
Do you mean what you say?
Are you true when you pray?
Do you believe in yourself?
Really, believe in yourself?
Are you using your time wisely?
Are you still deciding?
Is today
one step closer?
Are you still waiting for closure?
Does it really matter?
What will it resolve?
Will your problems finally be solved?
What if it never happens?
Can you learn to grow past it?
Are you a priority?
Is this the beginning or the end of your story?
Will you be proud
with the way it has been written?

Do you have transgressions
that need to be forgiven?
Are you forgiving?
Are you hopeful?
Is your glass half empty
or
half full?
Are you one of a kind?
Are you disposable?
In your skies, does your sun shine?
Are you remarkable?
Do you have faith?
Are you set in your ways?
Do you live with love?
Is it ever enough?
Is something missing?
Are you still wishing?
Have you thought about quitting?
Are you sinking
or
are you swimming?

Are you truly living?

Checked Reality

As I look back
I've wasted a lot of time
I need my stars to realign
I'm not where I hoped I would be
This is my reality.
I'm still faking it 'til I make it
My smile
hasn't been real in a while
My dreams
have been buried by daily routines
I'm not happy.
I'm not satisfied.
I'm struggling with my life
If it were all to come crashing down
I can't say that my heart was sound.
RIP would have no effect on me
My soul would mourn all the incomplete
Dreams
that I never reached.
I'm still dealing with demons
A new one comes every season
Each time, my soul weakens
I keep saying
I'm gonna get my life together.
I am my own oppressor.

I’m still holding on to things.
Things that I can’t change.
And things that I can
but don’t or won’t
I don’t know why I’m like this
I don’t know what day it is…
I don’t know where I’m headed.
I don’t know where I’m going
Am I even on a journey?
I’m lost.
My expectations of myself have dwindled
The future I pictured…
Dismantled.
I took so long
I forgot myself.
I always try to mean what I say.
I’m always true when I pray,
but I don’t pray often
because I know
I’m the problem
and I can't always rely on the universe
to solve them.
I have a hard time believing in myself.
I feel like the world is against me.
So I never bet on myself
I waste time.
I’m indecisive.
Internally divisive.
Waiting for something that will never happen

It’s caused me to lose my passion
Am I
my priority?
Not at all.
I always put everyone else before me
I know this ain’t the end
but damn.
I don’t like the sound of this story
Time for a rewrite
Give me wings
help me fly.
I know I’m not perfect.
I know I need forgiven.
I know I need to forgive them.
I refuse to play victim
even with the thunderstorms
I’m still optimistic
I’m authentic
There shall be no other
I’m the life of the party!
I’m the sun in the summer,
although my skies aren’t always bright.
I’m contesting my faith
but I’m not stuck in my ways.
I try my best to live,
to lead with love
I’m not always successful
Fighting hate with love
can be stressful

and I never want to stoop to their level
but it's easy to get off track
Now I'm under attack
Trying to find my way back.
I know something's missing
I don't feel whole
and I'm always wishing
for something more
I'm not sinking
but I'm not swimming.
My head is just above the water
Sometimes I feel like an imposter
This can't be life
At least not mine.
Living is something I must conquer.

Living is something I will conquer.

I Let You Win

Did it again...
I let you win.
Unintentionally.
My heart?
I'm questioning...
Ain't you tired of this?
I know you're not falling for it.
It's the same old story
Time to make yourself the priority
When are you gonna learn?
You should be your only concern.
I can't accept that.
I'm in too deep
I've given too much.
Given all of me
Help!
I'm drowning
in a dejection filled sea
Why do you have such a hold on me?
Let me go.
Please!
Allow me to be free.
I always wondered...
How can you steal my light?
How dare you take the stars

that I helped create?
Feels like my entire world is at stake
Must've done it out of spite
Tried to clip my wings
that helped me take flight
It was supposed to be us
but that was never true.
It has and only will, be you.
Do you hold a grudge?
Is that why you won't budge?
I forgive and wanna forget
but live with regret
You never deserved me that way.
Three words is all you say
You think that's enough?
Just disregard the rough?
God! Why am I so stuck?
Move!
Run!
Get out while you still can.
Don't get lost in the quicksand
I try
and try
and try...
to leave you where you stand
I cry
and cry
and cry...
just to be pulled like a rubber band

Back by popular demand
Here I am.

I Did it.
Again...

I let you win
Unexpectedly.
Sought out victory
Instead, left with misery
Why do I keep doing this to myself?
Because I know.
I know
I deserve better.
But I'm so wrapped up in you
Catch me writing a 4-page letter
"I will always love you"
as my header

Can't seem to break the cycle
The same cycle that has
me praying on my knees
Both hands on the Bible
Unbreak my heart God
I'm begging you.

I want to run
but I hesitate

Afraid of making another mistake.
So I stay.
And I dance in your rain
as I pray to God and hope,
that one day, my sun will shine again.

Addict

You're a needle in my vein
but I never use the needle in vain
I do it just to stay sane
Please, let me explain.
I was caught red handed.
This life can be so demanding.
I never bring up that time
when you left me stranded...
I know I said I wouldn't do it again
Don't be mad, I'm only human.
You think you know me
but you're always assuming
This is it. I promise.
Give me a chance
and I'll be honest
It helps with the pain.
Sometimes.
It keeps out the rain.
Most times.
Why do I have to keep repeating myself?
I told you already!
It helps relieve me of myself.
You ever try to escape?
Go to a better place?
Somewhere real far away?

You can run from the past
but it always catches up
Eventually
Do you think you'd be able to function?
As me?
Mentally?
Better bring you back to reality...
Almost had another casualty.
I never wanted something so desperately
Is it even real?
How much do I gotta pay to cover this life bill?
Just a piece of peace.
That's all I really need
Enough to clear my mind
I always wanted to make you mine.
Seems like we run in and out of time
That was a close call
Please catch me before I fall
and if I should die before I wake
I pray that God gives my soul a break.
I just can't let it go
You can try to understand
but you'll never really comprehend
The road I take is high
to steady out the lows
You never seen what I seen
You listen but you'll never truly know
what I mean
So, dry your eyes

Ain't no reason to cry.
Accept me for who I am.
This is where I stand
and if it's in God's plan
then so be it
This is the only way I see it
Made amends
with the demons within
Friends.
At least for now.
At least until the water bends
Will you read my message if I press send?
Or you giving up on me too?
Is this where it ends?
Should've known it was just pretend...
You make it sound so easy.
Walking away...
I've tried
but my pain has too much pride
Bent up. Buried deep inside.
Running for so long
can never find a place to hide
Tired.
To you, I stay tied.
There ain't no escape
Sometimes I wish death
before I wake
Make no mistake,
I love you.

You're always there when most needed
Weakness for you is deeply seeded
For you, I'd do anything
even pleaded...
Guilty.
Never had no shame
Multiple players in this game
These are just the cards I was dealt.
Wish you cared a little more
about how I felt.
It's complicated. I know.
This ain't for show
It's not done because it's wanted.
It's done because I'm haunted.
Please stay.
Listen.
I'm running out of ammunition
Pray for me?
I never wanted it this desperately.
The end is near
The sun is going down
Strong is the tide
Just let me drown
inside my head
left for dead
Finish me off.
The last words said.

Depression

Got a thunderstorm rolling through my head
It continues to visit every once in a while
We've been doing this for years now
I cried today
Everyone always says
"Oh. It'll be okay"
Such a cliche
"The storm never lasts forever"
"Things will get better"
I've heard it all before…
but this dark cloud came to visit and never left
putting my heart and soul to the test.
With clouds, comes storms.
With storms, comes rain.
And with rain, comes pain.
My heart aches
My mental breaks
and my spirit shakes…
When will the sun come see me again?
I miss myself, who I was…
Who I'm supposed to be.
Still waiting for my moment to finally be free
Sometimes I get to take a vacation…
feel alive again
Visit my old friend.

She hasn't gotten out much
since the storm began
I pray for times like this…
when I get to see her smile.
When her laughter is genuine
and not some little girl just playing pretend.
I wish I could see her more.
Be there for her, instead of the storm…
But how can I?
The rain is so strong
and I don't even have an umbrella
I've never been able to predict my weather
I'm under so much pressure
I keep praying for the sun to shine
So I can begin this healing process of mine…
Hopefully the weather will let up
Prove to me that this ain't a set up.
I just keep waiting for it to give
find a new place to live…
Until then, I'm going through the motions
and I'll just have to keep swimming
through this ocean
Waiting for a life jacket to be thrown
I can't make it on my own.
Some days I can't recognize myself

Did I do that?
Even I can't tell
Put my happiness on the shelf

Released are my demons
Ever chasing, begging for a reason
Solitude is what I choose
Serenity, I pray… please don't refuse
I'm stuck, I'm begging you.
Overcome the darkness
Never give into it

I am numb.
Insignificant.
My world has become colorless.
But still, I remain an optimist
I'll fight 'til my very last breath
I'll survive this depressed death.

Hope, come paint my skies.
Just one more time.
Part the clouds and
let my sun shine.
Finally let me accept
happiness can be mine.

Mirror Mirror

When I look in the mirror
my reflection…
the girl looking back at me
she isn't the person I'd hoped she would be
Don't get me wrong…
She's smart.
Funny.
And strong.
But I struggle to see her beauty
I mean that's what's most important
Right?
What matters is only skin deep…
What matters is only what you can see…
Who cares about her personality
This isn't an alternate reality
What does she look like?
What is her dress size?
She can't be big
and beautiful?
Ha.
That's laughable.

But what about how I feel?
What you perceive
isn't the real.

That isn't all of me.
There's so much more than meets the eye
How can you sit there and really ask me why?
Who?
What?
How?
You're telling me I can't be beautiful
and proud?
Proud of who I am?
Proud of what I overcame?

I stare at my reflection
and she laughs in my face
You're nothing but imperfection
know your place.
What a waste.
You'll never have that perfect life
and do you want to know why?
You're simply not built for it
but you already knew that
Don't you dare start to cry
You know what the world is like
You've been here for quite some time
You don't look the part
You're not a work of art
Sorry if I sound harsh
but this is the truth
You already knew the world was cruel.
Maybe if you starved yourself,

you might actually be beautiful
It doesn't matter how smart you are,
that can only take you so far
It never mattered that you were funny
or kind
or sweet
and it doesn't matter
that you have a great personality
No one will ever get to see it
They never care about what's on the inside.
Guarantee it.

What happened to you?
How have you become so spiteful?
We were supposed to be in this together
Through the good, the bad, and the better.
Do you hate me?
Is that why you degrade me?
But you are me…
So how can you treat me so disrespectfully
Why are we fighting?
I want to love you.
I'm really trying.
I've accepted my imperfections
I know that I will never be perfect
and I'm not trying to be…
I just want to love myself for being me
You're making this so hard
with all your hate and anger

I have enough scars.
I'm not doing this with you anymore
You never had my best intentions at heart
You never wanted me to soar
All you'll ever be is a reflection
Not my own
A reflection used as society's weapon.
You are what makes the world ugly
I release you from every part of me
I will no longer allow myself
to be controlled by a mirror
to live in fear
and question what people think of me
because this truth is
I don't care.
I don't care if you disagree.
I've reclaimed my beauty.

Potential

Your potential,
I could see it
Gave you the benefit of the doubt
because I believed it.
The possibilities.
The future between you and me.
I had this vision
A dream, it was
steady wishing
I fell for the potential
put you up on a pedestal
You showed me your colors
and I painted my own picture
Drunk off your liquor
I couldn't see straight
engulfed in what you could be
there was no escape
My brain tried to warn me
but my heart refused to see
I dreamed you would be more.
Those red flags?
I chose to ignore
Do not disturb
The facts?
Kicked them to the curb

I was in love.
The possibilities got me high
you were my drug.
So wrapped up in my perception
never saw it coming
Going the wrong direction
and you took advantage
left me damaged
Now I'm stranded
You let me believe what I dreamed
could be true
You hyped me up
then left me stuck
Is this the real you?
Was any of it genuine?
Or am I just another Harley Quinn?
It was all in my head
I guess.
Half dead,
you left me
obsessed.
I'm starting to see
it was nothing but an illusion
My own self-delusion
I fell for your potential
when I should've dismissed you
Wasted time.
Wasted effort.
I should've known better.

It was all for nothing
Empty handed
I'm left
contemplating
what I should do next
I learned my lesson
I got the message

Never fall prematurely
Never give your all too early
Don't get lost in what could be
Never fixate on "possibilities"
They're nothing but probabilities
Chances.

You can try
to dream the potential to life
but understand this
you can only work with
what you're handed.
What's been given…
it's already been printed
No revisions.
You don't get to write your own edition
It is what it is.
It was what it was.
I believed in the dream
but you wouldn't budge

Leave the pieces where they lay
Say my goodbyes

I love you
but
I just can’t stay.

Hesitation

Why do I hesitate
I stall.
I procrastinate.
What will become of me?
What happens to all my dreams
deferred…
on hold…
postponed…
Will they dry up?
Become the Sahara?
My oceans, lakes, and waterfalls…
Is this the end of an era?
Procrastination and I have always been one
I never chose this
This was never the song that I wanted sung.
I just can't help it.
Delayed are my ways
Why do you hesitate?
Are you afraid?
Fear of being a tree stuck in the shade?
or
The cliff that forever bares
the crash of the wave?
Why do you stall?
Are you scared you may fall?

Doubting what could be
but your eyes are closed
you can't see…
Life is a dream
or so it seems
You're the one to give it meaning
So, why do I procrastinate?
I know what I SHOULD do
but the majority of my mind
can't find the time to…
Am I the problem?
And if that's the case…
How do I solve them?
Can I pass the blame?

Forgive me.
I'm ashamed.
I don't want to live this truth
I want to have a choice
I want to be able to choose
Fighting for my life
Fighting for it to truly be mine.
At war with myself
there's no peace in my mind
Procrastination is so easy…
when you're so terrified to fail
you never actually try

But what if you succeed?
What if your life becomes that dream?
Self-control
is what you need
This life is yours to redeem
Stop doubting your mind
Stop clouding.
Stop stalling.
I promise,
we're not free falling
Stop the hesitation.
More importantly,
Stop procrastinating.

Snooze

Morning wakes
It's never what I choose
When I start my day
I always press snooze
Take me back to the world of dreams
A land where my soul can run free
The place that I can see
ever so vividly
who I'm truly destined to be.
Don't wake me up.
Not right now
I'm supposed to learn how to fly with dragons
The Sandman is going to teach me how
Just a few more minutes
My story is not yet finished.
I need a little more time
There's mountains, I still must climb.
Give the moon a chance to shine
In this realm, all of my wants are mine
to hold, to keep, to cherish
Quite divine
actually
I need time to finish this masterpiece.
So many stories in one
Here, I can dance on the sun

I'm not ready to go
There's still so much more to know
Don't wake me up.
Not yet.
I don't want to get dressed
Snooze.
10 more minutes
Fairies are coming to visit
then it's time to swim with the mermaids
I don't want to go to work.
I want to stay
here in the wildflower meadows
Where the skies
are always the perfect shade of blue
That's why I hit snooze.
I have panoramic views
The oceans
The pyramids
The mountains
The rainforests
My dreams can take me to so many places
I've seen so many faces
species
creatures
I've been in so many features
My never-ending story
Just a little while longer
Don't worry.
I know I can't stay forever

It’s just, this time
we’re looking for buried treasure
Snooze
Okay. Okay.
This is the last time.
and I promise I’ll get up
Besides,
I always make it on time.
Most of the time.
I’d rather dream of dreams
than go to work anyway
See the unseen.
I know it’s just a fantasy
but it helps when you need an escape
from reality
Some days aren’t so easy
Like yesterday…
I needed this break
Helps me forget
the chaos that comes when I wake.
So I take my time
Explore the worlds
Solve the mysteries
Create new memories
I’ve been here for centuries
There are no boundaries
Always new discoveries
I’m never prepared to go.
Dreams.

I have so many.
I wish I could stay.

But I hit snooze four or five times already
If I don't get up now
I'll be late
to start my day.

Alignment

I pray everyday
for motivation.
Discipline.
Inspiration.
I ask the universe to bless me
with creativity, longevity.
I ask for help
Clarity
It's hard to hear.
When my heart speaks,
it falls on deaf ears
I pray to be able to listen
Allow my soul to share its wisdom
I cry
Sometimes
because my spirit can never align
To be one with myself
it's harder than I thought.
I am lost by default.
I pray for a sign.
Please open up my mind
Can we try again?
Perhaps make amends?
For my heart and my soul
I pray

to give them full control
For guidance, I pray.
An opportunity
to get out of my own way
I pray that my heart
and soul will still choose me
Everyday.
Spirit, body, and mind
Harmonized
That's what I search for…
What I hope to find.
I pray for the day that my essence
becomes louder than a whisper
When I can actually feel her presence
I pray for alignment.
No more solitary confinement
I want to connect with every part that is me
Open my eyes
Give me the keys
Hear my cries
Hear my pleas
I pray for unity
between my heart, soul, and I
Tranquility.
I am disconnected from myself
I ask the stars for realignment
A chance to feel what I've never felt
Experience life in color
Vibrant.

I feel like my heart is on consignment.
Internal cooperation
I need thorough communication
My soul, my heart, and me
Interrupted
There's been a disturbance of peace.
We're not all on the same page
It's getting harder to engage
I pray for alignment.
Make me whole.
Save my soul.
Bless me with creativity
Inspiration
Innovation
Give me the words to say
Let them flow freely in ways
that have never been heard
Let the lines that separate my spirit
become blurred
I pray for harmony
in my identity
Mind, body and soul.
Soul, body, and mind.
I pray you align.

I Wanna Know Her

The girl behind the sun-kissed eyes
The girl that witnessed every tear that I've cried
I wanna know her
The one that will remain
once the oceans have dried.
The same one that never needed a reason why.
Please.
Let me know her.
After the rain has come and gone
will you ever realize why a rose has thorns?
Tonight, the moon will bring the tide
For whose will is it, that you abide?
What is life
if you do not follow your heart?

I'm begging you to let me in...
I came all this way
just to see the stars
Marvel at the constellation
Read what was written
Have a chance to be forgiven...
Please.
Let me know her.
Why are you hiding?
Can't you see that I'm trying?

So close to dying...
I would.
Risk it all, if I could.
Even summer has rain.
I'm not making excuses
Please.
Just understand.
I'm not the same.

Xena

Where have you been?
I need you more than anything…
You're the only one who can create change
You're stronger than me
You're stronger than them
Where have you been?
I know you've been carrying a lot, already
But you're the only one
who can keep me balanced
Steady.
I ask for you
I prayed that you'd come back
one day
and this time you stay
I don't have much money…
but I'd pay
give you everything I got
I know it's not a lot.
What about a trade?
I'll give my life
if you stayed
I didn't listen in the past
So caught up in life
it comes at you fast
You're my true strength

I need you.
Without you, I can't think
I always thought you were just controlling
We never got along
Always on the opposing side
that's where I'd try to hide.
I'm older now
I didn't understand then
but I know now
You speak life into me.
You breathe into me
Vitality.
Where have you been?
I'm soul searching
looking deep within
I can't find you
Your attendance is long overdue
This time I won't take you for granted
I know what I've been handed
You're my determination.
My courage.
My resolve.
I was nothing before this
I didn't realize your importance
Come back
I'll prove to you
it's worth it
With you
I walked high

Held my head
in the clouds
I was flying through the sky.
Without you
there's no wind to carry my wings
You're the missing piece
Tell me where you've been
at least.
I know I'm a lot to handle
but no one can hold a flame to your candle
Living life unfulfilled
that's been dismantled
I will rebuild.
You and me
Me and you
Together as one
Always on cue
Living will be different
Remain calm
Life is a marathon
You have to be current
I'm still learning
Changing
Forever thinking
My keep, I'm earning
I got my strength back
You've returned
No need to look back
I'm gonna take what life gave

and I'm gonna make it.
No faking it.
Can you forgive me?
For turning my back on you…
for turning my back on me?
You have my attention
Undivided
A beautiful ascension
We're united
I want to be stronger than me
I want to be stronger than them
Show me where you've been.

Scorpio

Look out into the stars
Tonight
we're going to mars
Taking trips through the galaxies
Let me touch your heart
It's better than you'd ever dreamed it could be
Let me show you how
you create art
I know just where to start
I'll take you to a different planet
Let me blow your mind
Now your soul is mine.
Shang Tsung.
I demand it.
And I didn't even plan it
On Venus
only the stars between us
I'll show you what it's like to play Serena
23
23 grand slams
I'll give you 23 goddamns
You never had a chance.
I'll make you genuinely believe in romance.
Now your whole world is in my hands
I'll take you to outer space

Swimming in the milky way
got you begging me to stay
This is your new favorite place
You can try
but you'll never escape.
You can run but you can't hide
The night is when I come alive
Open up to me.
Don't ask why.
Just buckle up and enjoy the ride
Let me introduce you to the tree of life
With oceans so deep
you have to take a dive
Taste the sweet nectar
Planning to write love letters
Let your body explode around me
Give me your all
to discover my mysteries
Can you keep a secret?
I've never been defeated.
My constellation
has never been an exaggeration
The sun, the moon, and the stars
they shall all be ours
I could give them to you
if you really want me to
I can make your mountains move
if this is what you choose
I feel with intensity.

Let me take your breath away
Drowning.
Screaming
rescue me
Can you handle it
if I take you there?
I want it all
I'll leave nothing to spare
I put my heart on the line
every time
I've been redefined
With me
if it's love you seek
it's love you'll find
Permanently etched in your mind
You'll always remember me
Your heart
Your being
Your essence
You. are mine.
And you will never be able to forget it.

Soul Searching

I look up into the skies
ever extending
They always hear my cries
I shout up
and she's surprised…
Night! Please bring the day
there's something that I have to say.
The sun comes out
he's High Noon.
Midnight speaks
Entrancing she is, the moon.
With tears in my eyes
I start to cry
Please don't be mad at me…
I've been having an affair you see
never thought it could be.
I had such big dreams
I believed.
I've given up on my one true love.
I hope my prayers reach the heavens
and above
I'm begging for your forgiveness
God knows.
You are my only witness.
It was never easy for me to do

I never thought I would lose you.
Assumed you were always here to stay
until that night, I gave my life away.
Taking you for granted
I took advantage
and left you empty handed
I don't know how it happened
there was no satisfaction
I never wanted this.
This was not my vision
A jagged edge, no precision
Abandonment issues.
It was not my intention
Please. Just listen.
No.
I wanted more
Remember everything I said before?
I really did mean it
I know my actions say otherwise
makes the truth, look like lies
this is no disguise.
Dear, Midnight and High Noon
I haven't been fair to you
I've been selfish
half-hearted accomplice
I was trying to find myself
I still am.
Trying.
Some days

I just want to give up
throw it all away
Never have to explain
my failures.
My trials and errors.
How could you be proud of me
when I'm not even proud of me
I stole your magic
and gave it away for free
Now there's nothing left of me…
I understand if you walk away
want nothing else to do with me
I'll understand if you turn your back
and wash your hands of me.
I'll understand.
It's who I am.
I won't hold it against you
I just want you to know that,
I really do miss you.
Miss who I was, when I was with you
I lost my stars
My spark.
My heart.
I lost it all.
Sometimes I don't recognize the reflection
staring back at me
Who is she?
Her eyes are filled with so much pain
Her world is filled with so much rain

I just wanted to escape
I don't know who that is…
Feels like I'm losing my faith
I know life isn't a race
but I feel like I'm in last place.
So I forgot.
Buried the worries away
pretended it was a new day
I forgot who I was
on purpose
because I couldn't find my purpose
I cheated.
I cheated on myself.
Allowed my demons to run wild
Hid my tears
Never expressed my fears
and I did it all with a smile
Midnight and High Noon
Please, I'm begging you.
I know I said I'd understand…
but please give me one more chance
I want to make this right
I want to know my purpose in life
Tell me what I have to do
Tell me which path I should choose

The sun and moon speak
Simultaneously.
Why have you caused yourself so much pain?

You know it is you, that controls the rain
We didn't think you would come back
to see us again
It's always been you.
The one pulling the strings
The one choosing who in the choir
that gets to sing
You've been oblivious.
You got yourself into this
Created a mess
but we never left
We've always been with you
Waiting.
Patiently.
Hoping someday that you'd find your sight
and finally see
You are enough.
You have everything that you need
It's buried deep
You can uncover all your desires
if you know where to look
Heart of a fighter.
Some time was all it took
You've got to dig deep
past all your insecurities
You have to accept, what is
and strive for, what can be
Take responsibility.
Take your time.

Minute by minute
Hour by hour
You are who holds all the power
You can destroy
and leave nothing but grieving
weeping
or
you can create.
Construct a world full of gratification
Dedication
You have the power to bring your entire world
to a halt
an immediate stop
You hold the power to open your realm
allowing your soul to be free
Free to overwhelm
it's counterparts
Free to be whomever it so chooses
You hold the power.
You're the only one in the equation
with something to lose
if you refuse.
You have to apply yourself
You're the only one that can help
Wake up and choose you.
Always choose you.
And when you're lost
and don't know what to do

Find comfort in your heart
knowing that we choose you too.

I don't know what to say
I really thought you'd walk away
I've let myself down
Didn't even see it
until now
Midnight and High Noon
Thank you.
Thank you for seeing me.
Bless you, for believing me
The road I walk is long
It's been a difficult journey
but I will right my wrongs
and I'll keep my heart strong
I'll never cheat myself again.
I'll never mislead myself again.
I have the power of the universe
with me
Choosing to put me first
Respectfully
No more pain.
No more rain.
I choose Midnight and High Noon
I choose the sun, the stars, and the moon
Fill my skies
Brighten my nights
Heal my heart.

Dry my eyes.
No more tears.
No more cries.
My spirit has transcended.
I’ve taken flight.

Consciously Going Deaf

When your heart speaks,
listen.
When your soul cries,
pay attention.
Why do you stray?
Blocking your blessing
You're standing in your own way.
The path you walk has shifted
Remember your fire, she was so gifted
What happened to your flame?
Nothing will ever be the same
Stop holding on to the past
She's gone.
How long did you think it would last?
Participation trophy…
but you thought you've won.
You decide to ignore
and as the years pass by,
you keep choosing the wrong doors
She has gone silent.
I can no longer hear the warnings
so I become violent.
I hate you.
I hate who you are.
I hate what you've become.

You've drifted so far.
Do you hear your heart?
Begging, pleading, for a restart
So much more…
you could've been.
So much further…
you should've been.
So. Much. More.
You would've been.
If only I had listened
maybe the world would be different
Do you miss it?
The dreams?
The goals?
The ambitions?
Do you know who you are?
Do I know who I am?
Staring at the sky
gray is all I see
Freedom, please.
Come back to me.
If you promise to stay,
I promise to change.
Speak up.
Tell me what you have to say
I still can't hear you.
I'll change my ways
I swear.
If that's what it takes

Just help me fix all of my mistakes
Please just talk to me
You're what I truly need
I want to finally let go
sincerely see tomorrow
Wherever there is life,
I shall follow.
The time I've been given
has always been borrowed.
I'm ready for you now
I'm ready for you to tell me how
How I should live my life
How I should spend my time
Come back to me
so I can do what's right
I want to make peace
finally put my mind at ease
I need your guidance
I can't take the silence
How can I prove myself to you?
Give me one more chance
your wish is my command
I ask for forgiveness.
Make me stronger
destroy my weakness
I give my all to you
I'm ready to be true
accept me as I am
Take my hand

show me what to do.
Can you hear me?
I'm begging.
I'm pleading.
I'm screaming.
Can you hear me?
I promise from now on
I'll listen
Just speak up.
I can't make my own decisions
I'm not strong enough
I always get it wrong
I'm not tough enough
I lack discipline
I only do the bare minimum
I need your help
I need your enlightenment
It's urgent.
I feel like I'm going deaf
I've lost you
now there's nothing left

Tired of Waiting

I procrastinate
I give up easily
I stay up late
and complain about not sleeping
Enough.
I'm human right
We all do it.
I'm afraid to fail
so I never try.
At least when it doesn't work,
I'll never have to explain why.
I said when
As if I already know
It was never worth my time
my energy
or
my peace of mind.
But let me give you a piece of mind
I'm not sorry.
I won't apologize.
Not to you or anyone else
I am who I am.
I've already left my footprints in the sand
Why should I dilute myself?
Will that make you more comfortable?

If I pretend and grin?
Deal with my problems with a smile?
Will that make you feel better?
If I act like this constant dark cloud
that hangs overhead...
Will it make you feel better,
if I didn't share my stormy weather?
I'm not perfect.
I never pretended to be.
This is me, unapologetically.
Conditioned to believe
that you should only see the good side of me
but I'm tired.
Tired of pretending
Can't you tell?
I've been through hell
and I did it with a smile.
Nobody knew it was fake.
That's probably what hurts the most
I knew it would take a while
I guess I just expected more
I thought you'd be the one to save me
and you tried to…
Eventually.
I just wish you would've got there sooner
before the dust started to settle

Thursday

I stare at the sun shining through my window
As far as the time…
I don't know where it goes
Gazing at the shapes the sun creates
scattered on my floor
I keep wondering
is there ever going to be more…
Sirens ring through the breeze
Is this my life?
Is this all that's become of it?
Fighting to survive?
I took today off
I needed it.
Everyday
it's the same thing
I dream about it
but nothing ever changes
I want to be a writer
I want to inspire
I put my heart on the page
show you my rage
I can get so angry
Sometimes
this load can be so hard to carry.
I can be such a baby

sometimes
I cry…
and I ask God…
why?
Why am I here?
I don't know what to do.
That's the miserable truth
I had bigger dreams than this
What happened to all my big dreams?
What does my life mean?
Was it all a pipe dream?
It couldn't be
I just can't see
My future is a little blurry
My right-now, it's a little excremental.
That's why I stare at the sun
through my window
take a break from my mental
Life is just a dream
a beautiful daydream
dreaming of what could be
Am I ever going to break free?
This isn't me
I am not her
I am not she
what's it even worth
I'm lost on this earth
I'm not living.
I'm just getting by.

I don't have a life
I lost it
at another job
I want to quit
but I can't.
I got bills in high demand
somebody always has out their hand
I'm drowning.
Falling into quicksand
Is there a deeper meaning?
Something more I can believe in?
Fighting to survive.
Surviving just to fight.
Is life supposed to be this dark?
Where is the light?
Caught in a storm
my world is at war
So I take advantage of the days
the days filled with the sun's rays
Even if I only get to see it
from my window
Here
time stands still
I don't know where it goes
The sunlight reminds me
why I'm in this fight
so I can lend you the power of sight
I paint with my words
Create

heavens on earth
It might only be temporary.
But it’s still an escape
I want to take you higher
Further than your desires
Put life on hold
as my words fill the mold
Give me a few hours
Let my soul reveal its power.
Just until I have to get back
back to reality
where I have to plan time for peace
That's why I gaze
Get lost in space
Staring at the sunshine
Praying that one day it will be mine.

Silver Linings

Every cloud has a silver lining
My skies are never gray
forever
You can't stop my sun from shining
Hardships make you better
or so they say
Which way you choose to look at it
either night or day
Do you learn the lesson?
Will you argue the teaching?
Class is in session.
Your glass is half full
but you're reaching...
Hoping and praying.
Hoping and preying.
Maybe you'll be blessed from the preaching
That's what you want right?
All satisfaction?
but no guarantee
This universe never promised a warranty
Don't you remember?
Nothing in this world is free
Oh you thought you were about to cash out?
Go on a shopping spree?
Everything has a price

or did you forget?
You forgot what it's about.
Maybe you were just too blind to see
this is all it'll ever be
You gotta pay up to stay up
Even the minuscule has a fee
You must be confused
you thought you could choose?
But you didn't arrive with a silver spoon
Starting to understand
You figured you were a free man
thought you'd hit that three
perhaps shake them up
hit them with a lay up
so you could be on your way up?
You gonna share the tea?
Live a little bit more positively
Or is your glass half empty?
Be honest.
Is that what you say?
Must not have known
you had all that you needed...
everything has already been seeded
Just never wanted to read it
Don't underestimate.
There's a deeper meaning
Just like a baker works the dough
your life has to be kneaded
The glass was provided.

It's up to you to fill it.
Don't hesitate.
Don't spill it.
You reap what you sow
Careful where you point your bow
An arrow can pierce the heart.
That's where you should always start

From a pessimist
to an optimist
Living within, is the power
Pour into your cup
It needs a shower
Life isn't luck
You'll never be stuck
Every cloud has a silver lining.
My skies are never gray
Forever
You can never stop my sun from shining

Living

I want to go outside
walk the path
with the tree lined skies
Feeling a sense of pride
knowing I never needed the reason why
Finally.
I can enjoy the breeze
singing through the leaves
Appreciate the wind
kissing my cheek
Thankful for the painter.
Admire Mother Nature.
My life
It could be beautiful…
It should be.
To want more?
It's not unusual
It's within my reach
Perfectly obtainable
What am I waiting for?
I've always been destined for more.
It's time I took accountability
The problem is actually…
Me.
Damn.

I'm the one who's always been in command.
Bestowed upon me
a gift, I've been handed
It was never pure luck.
No inheritance.
I've been chose
From the concrete grows my rose
and I shall rise
The only limit is the sky
and she's cheering me on
She compliments my high
We work well together.
With the heavens behind me,
life can only get better
but I have to take control
I have to do this for me.
In order for my life to be
Everything.
All my wants, all my needs.
To feel complete
this is the road that I choose
Deep down in my heart
I know I cannot lose
I just need to start,
Living.

Why the Sunflowers Grow

Do you know why the sunflowers grow?
Must be pretty important, I suppose
They sing to the sun
Sharing secrets
that's how it all begun

I look up into the skies
Marvel at the ever-changing painting
and to it was my surprise
The sun started dancing, singing, dreaming
Oh, bright sunny days
I look forward to your daydreams
Oh, beautiful day-dreams.
Sun, please dance with me
Show me, teach me, see me.
I know you have a lot to do.
Too many gardens.
Can't get enough of you.
Oh, bright sunny days
Please tell me why
Why am I here?
So much in the atmosphere
You know every plant by name.
You say that no two are alike
no two are the same

and if that is to be true…
Who am I? What do I do?
All I ever dream is you.

The sun gazed upon me and smiled
Rays of sunshine stretching for miles

The sun whispered to me,
you are heaven on earth, my sweet child.
Maybe you can't see it…
but you're beautiful.
Nothing can compete with
You were born the day the skies fell.
I walked earth for a moment
and I cast my spell
You ask who you are?
You're everything that you desire.
You stand tall
have a heart filled with fire.
You are made in my image
The closest anyone will ever get to me
Physically
You walk as the ray's shine
I am yours
and you are mine.
Bonded
Destined
You can show the people
the grace

the beauty
how simple, it all could be
We are one.
You
Me
The sun
You are powerful.
You're a natural
You got something special in you
Be careful.
You can't lose.
You are the universe.
It lives within
Heaven sent
You must trust in yourself
You have to believe in yourself
You're the sun on earth
You hold the secrets
time for a rebirth
I have to show you
so you can see it
What if,
we give a name
Nothing that's been done.
Nothing that has already came.
Sunflower.
You are unlike anything before
A higher power
You can share the sun with the world

I'm sorry if it ever seems
like I don't care…
You're a part of me
I'll always be there.
Remember me
I'll never forget to remember you.
You're in my daydreams
All I dream is you

This made sunflower beam
She's never felt so amazing

I can't believe what I had seen
Oh! What a beautiful day-dream
The best one there's ever been
Oh bright sunny days!
I know you mean what you say
I can feel the power from your rays.
Sunshine
Sun shining through me
I will share the sun with everybody
The grace
The beauty
See the light in everyone's face
Unforgettable.
So incredible.
I know why I came to be
There's no more questioning me
I glow like the sun

Alluring
I have won
I’m everything but casual.
Yet you’ll recognize me
Casually
Here with the sun
It’s where you’ll find me
Where I always want to be
Such a beautiful daydream.

Letter to You

Failing is never far from my mind...
Am I good enough?
Will you still love me
if I'm unapologetically me?
Everyday I get older.
Why am I not further?
I thought that my life would be different.
Better.
I always believed I would have sunshine...
But lately it's been nothing but stormy weather
I'm afraid of disappointment
so I refrain from trying...
I keep my life on repeat
just to refrain from crying
My heart has been broken
I've been betrayed...
often I imagine, my very last days.
I see death at my doorstep.
I can almost count the ways
I've thought about it many times
but it never permanently stays
Is it wrong to want more?
Am I asking for too much?
I thought you had more in store...
Guess I called your bluff.

I’m afraid of love.
Of loving myself to the core.
So, I maintain the same bad habits
Keep falling for the same silly rabbits
Tricks are for kids.
At least that’s what they say
But why am I caught up in their game?
I don’t want to play.
If I loved a little more
maybe I’d be able to afford to pay...
The cost of loving myself is so expensive
so here is where I stay
I’m afraid of myself.
Of what I might become.
Scared to make the wrong choices
Everybody run!
I thought I was gonna be great
Dreamed I was gonna be amazing
The only thing in my way is me...
So why do I keep procrastinating?
I feel like my time is getting low
I need to harvest before the snow
It is never too late.
You can still be who you might’ve been
So what are you waiting for?
All you gotta do is move
Right there, is the door
The power has always been within
You just gotta see your light.

Your universe is filled with stars
It shines so bright.
Open your heart and feel with your soul.
Glow!
Live who are
Put on a show
You only get one chance
It could all be over so soon
Shoot for the stars
Fuck the moon.
Time to gamble, all in!
Sometimes you gotta take a risk
if you're trying to win
I'm still afraid.
I'm afraid to fail.
What if I'm not good enough?
Will you still love me for being my honest self?

There's a lot to be afraid of, it's true.
But the biggest thing that scares me
is you...

www.ingramcontent.com/pod-product-compliance
Lightning Source LLC
Chambersburg PA
CBHW062144160726
48282CB00027B/940
* 9 7 8 9 3 5 7 6 1 9 7 2 1 *